Why Choose Debt Settlement

Most consumers who seek help from settlement companies are unable to pay their debts. Usually they suffer from a financial hardship such as job or income loss, divorce, and health problems. Basically these consumers are incapable, rather than unwilling, to pay off their debts.

Debt settlement is a better option than consolidation loans, bankruptcy, or avoidance. Utilizing a debt settlement to pay off their debt, consumers are able to improve their debt-to-income ratio and have more control over the process of getting out of debt.

Example:

A client that has about $35,000 in credit card debt and is paying around $1200 in monthly credit card payments can have a new monthly program payment around $518 and typically can reduce their debt by about $21,000 becoming debt free in about 3 years.

Current Total Debt

$35,000.00

Total Savings

$21,000.00

I0473925

Current Monthly Payment

$1,200.00

New Monthly Payment

$518.00

COMMON OBJECTIONS

Damages credit - Credit reports will show evidence of debt settlements and the associated <u>FICO</u> scores will be lowered temporarily as a result. However, if a "paid in full" letter is obtained from the creditor, the debtor's credit report should show no sign of a debt settlement. Additionally, as debtors settle their accounts the score starts to go back up again.

Potential for lawsuits - Though few creditors wish to push borrowers toward bankruptcy, (and the potential of governmental protection against all debts), there's always the possibility of a <u>lawsuit</u> whenever debts lay unpaid. In the debt settlement process the debtor's accounts remain in default. While the debts are still in default the creditor or its assignee can still file a lawsuit against a debtor. Most creditors and debt collectors want a lump sum payment to settle for less than the full debt.

Eligibility of debts - In addition, the specific debts of the borrowers themselves affect the success of negotiations. <u>Tax liens</u> and domestic judgments, for reasons that should be clear, remain unaffected by attempts at settlement. Student loans, even those not federally subsidized, have been granted special powers by recent legislation to attach bank accounts without possibility of Chapter 7 bankruptcy protection. Also, some individual creditors, including Discover Card, for example, tend to have an aggressive resistance against negotiations.

WHAT IS DEBT SETTLEMENT

Do-it-yourself debt settlement

It is possible for a consumer to imitate the methods of professional debt settlement companies and many people report success in negotiating a debt settlement for themselves. Initiation of negotiations can begin by calling the customer service department of the credit card company. In general, the credit card company will only deal with a consumer when the consumer is behind on payments but capable of making a lump sum payment. A payment plan is not an option; the credit card company will demand that the consumer make a lump sum payment of the settlement amount.

Advantages

By negotiating debts on their own, debtors are able to save in fees that would otherwise be paid to a debt settlement company or an attorney. This option also gives the debtor more control over the process which may, or may not, be a motivational factor to continue successfully completing the process.

Disadvantages

Consumers may face difficulty getting through to decision makers or long delays in any negotiations or paperwork processing with the creditors. Furthermore, every creditor has different processes and procedures in how they determine settlement offers and terms. Not knowing those can leave a consumer in the dark. Settlement Companies have a Customer service department to assist consumers with any questions or difficulties that arise during their program. This support can be particularly valuable, especially in cases where creditors become aggressive. If an account were to escalate to legal status, a consumer settling on their own would need to seek out a third party for help. Unfamiliarity of the settlement process can be intimidating and mistakes can be made. You will need to beware of fine print and carefully review any correspondence, proposed settlement or agreement with a creditor. Settlement Agreements should be reviewed very carefully, perhaps by a third party, to make sure that all the terms are those that are agreed upon. Settling one's debt can be an emotionally draining and difficult process

Why Would a Creditor Settle for Less?

The creditor's primary incentive is to recover funds that would otherwise be lost if the debtor filed for bankruptcy. The other key incentive is that the creditor can often recover more funds than through other collection methods. Collection agencies and collection attorneys charge commissions as high as 40% on recovered funds. Bad debt purchasers buy portfolios of delinquent debts from creditors who give up on internal collection efforts and these bad debt purchasers pay between 1 and 12 cents on the dollar, depending on the age of the debt, with the oldest debts the cheapest. Collection calls and lawsuits sometimes push debtors into bankruptcy, in which case the creditor often recovers no funds.

Tax consequences - Another common objection to debt settlement is that debtors whose debts are partially canceled outside the bankruptcy system will need to report the canceled portion of the debt as taxable income. (IRS Publication Form 982) The Internal Revenue Service (IRS) considers any amount of forgiven debt as taxable income. The forgiving creditor must provide the taxpayer with a 1099-C tax form for amounts $600 or greater. This form will list the amount of forgiven debt and interest in Box 2. Taxpayers with portions of personal loans forgiven may not subtract the interest reported in Box 3 from the amount of reportable income on this form.

However, the IRS does not require taxpayers to report forgiven debt if the tax payer was insolvent at the time the creditor forgave the debt. Being insolvent means that the amount of a debtor's debts are greater than his/her assets (how much money and property the debtor owns). However, the IRS adds that "you cannot exclude any amount of canceled debt that is more than the amount by which you are insolvent."

For example, if a taxpayer is $10,000 in debt and owns $3,000 in assets, he/she cannot exclude more than $7,000 of forgiven debt from his/her income tax. Any forgiven debt over $7,000 that year must be reported as taxable income.

IDENTIFYING CREDITORS FOR THE PROGRAM

The first step in creating your successful debt settlement program is to determine how much unsecured debt you are dealing with, including credit card debt, department store cards, personal loans—"**any unsecured debt**"

What Does *Unsecured Debt* Mean? – In finance, **unsecured debt** refers to any type of debt or general obligation that is not collateralised by a lien on specific assets of the borrower in the case of a bankruptcy or liquidation or failure to meet the terms for repayment.

What Does SECURED DEBT Mean?
Debt backed or secured by collateral to reduce the risk associated with lending. An example would be a mortgage, your house is considered collateral towards the debt. If you default on repayment, the bank seizes your house, sells it and uses the proceeds to pay back the debt

The following is a list of types of debt that cannot be included into a debt settlement program.

- Credit Unions

- Government Debt (Student Loans)

- Time Shares

- Repossessions

- Short Sale

Please use the Identifying my creditor's worksheet to the right to make notes about your creditors.

Try to avoid a Bank Conflict

Create Your Plan

The first step to determine the best possible debt settlement plan for you is to figure out how much money you can afford each month to put into your savings account. You want this amount to be enough to get you out of debt within three years but also be enough you can afford each month.

Let's start by figuring out your budget. *(Use Budget Worksheet at the back of the book)*

Once budget worksheet is completed it's now time to figure out how much we are going to enrol in your debt settlement program, we are going to assume you are going to get a 60% reduction from the starting balance. Please use the provided space below to do the math to determine how much your monthly payments will be.

LETS DO SOME MATH!

Total Current Credit Card Payments: $_____
(Line 1)

Total Current Credit Card Debt: $_____
(Line 2)

(Multiply Line 2 X .40%)

New Projected Credit Card Debt: = $_____
(Line 3) <u>(40% of line 2)</u>

Total Savings: *(Subtract Lines 2 and 3)* = $_____
(Line 4)

Divide Line 2 by 36   (line 2 ÷ 36) = _____
36 Month Program *(Line 5)*

Divide Line 2 by 24   (line 2 ÷ 24) = _____
24 Month Program *(Line 6)*

Now based on your monthly budget you can make a decision on whether you are going to do a 36 month program or a 24 month program

What program are you going to choose? *(Write in areas below)*

My Monthly Payment is: $_____
The Number of Months I will deposit into
Savings is: _____ Months

I want you to write down some important data:

Your Current Payment is: *(Insert Line 1)*
$_____

Your New Monthly Payment is: *(Insert Line 5 or 6)*
$_____

Your Monthly Payment Savings are: *(Subtract Top 2 Lines)*
$_____

Your Current Credit Card Debt: *(Insert Line 2)*
$_____

Your New Projected Credit Card Debt: *(Insert Line 3)*
$_____

Your Total Credit Card Savings is: *(Subtract Top 2 Lines)*
$_____

SETTING UP YOUR ACCOUNT

It is imperative to the success of your settlement efforts that you set up a dedicated account that you use strictly to settle your cards. This way you are less likely to spend your settlement money on other expenses. It is proven that you are more likely to keep money in savings if you have it located at a bank completely separate from your primary account used to pay your bills.

Here are the simple steps to getting this set up:

1. Pick a bank that is not your primary bank to open your account

2. Make sure that you do not have any cards that you plan on settling located where you are opening your account

3. Once the account is open set up an auto transfer in the amount that you determined you would need to settle your debt

4. Avoid using the money in your dedicated savings account at all costs

GOING DELINQUENT

Going delinquent is a required set in the settlement process. Without going delinquent creditors have no incentive to settle for an amount that is less than you owe. This is one of the issues that the average consumer tends to have with credit card companies. We can't tell you how many times we have heard a consumer say, "I paid them on time every month, then when I fell on hard times and called them for help they stated they could not help me since I had been paying them on time." This backwards mind set from the creditors' perspective has caused hundreds of thousands of American's to turn to debt settlement.

Here are the steps to going delinquent:

1. With most creditors you will need to be 120 days delinquent before you will start to get good settlements from them

2. This delinquency process shows the creditor that your hardship is significant enough that you are unable to pay them the minimum monthly payments

3. Do not even pay a partial payment, this will slow down and impede the settlement process. If you are paying partial payments it shows that you will continue to pay monthly and they will still charge you late fees and increase your interest rate

SAVINGS REQUIREMENTS

There are things to remember when thinking about saving for settlements. You are going to want to get all of your debts together and see how many unsecured debts you are going to try and settle. You then want to figure out how much money you are spending on these debts currently per month. This will tell you what the **Current Situation** is.

For instance you may have 10 creditors that you are going to try and settle with and these cards may be costing you an average of $120 per month. This would mean that you are currently paying $1200 per month towards these credit cards.

You need to know your **Current Situation**, so that you can figure out what you will be able to save towards settlement. If the $1200 per month is not doable but you think that you can save $1000 per month towards settlement than you should do that. This would be a pretty aggressive plan and would have you debt free very quickly. However it may not be realistic. You need to make sure that what you decide to save per month towards settlement is a number that you can stick with. It is very important that you don't set yourself up for failure.

HANDLING CREDITOR CALLS

You can make this as easy or as hard as you choose to make it. <u>This can be a big stumbling block for the uninformed client</u>. Clients that are informed can move through this portion of the program very easily. Let me spell this out for you as simply as I can.

********DO NOT COMMUNICATE WITH CREDITORS!!********

This can be easier said than done. The temptation when you hear the phone ringing is to answer it. You may feel as though you are required to answer your phone. You may feel obligated to answer the phone when it rings. What you will need to understand is that you are not required to answer your telephone nor should you feel obligated. Just as when someone comes to the door there is no requirement to get the door, and in some instances it can even be dangerous to answer the door when not expecting company. <u>This needs to be the attitude that you adopt when it comes to phone calls.</u>

Remember when you decide to get out of debt and live a debt free life, it is not without some sacrifice. You have chosen a new path, a new way to take back control of your financial situation. On this new path you are in charge and it is up to you to make the best decisions possible. What you want to keep in mind as you start this process is that you are trying to gain leverage with your creditors so that they will settle with you. The only way to do this is to choose to stop making your payments on a monthly basis and instead choose to save this money towards settlement. Now the idea is not to **let the cat out of the bag** early in this process as this may speed up the collection efforts by the creditors. These creditors have internal departments to deal with consumers that are falling behind on their payments. For example they have 30 day late departments, 60 day late departments, 90 day late departments, and so on. So as you are saving money towards settlement you should allow them to go through their everyday normal internal process of dealing with clients that are behind on their payments. This will include calling you, sending you letters, and calling and calling and calling. What you are doing here is **buying yourself some time.** The idea here again is to not answer your phone, **invest in a caller ID**, change your phone number, or whatever works for you. Do not answer the phone and explain to the creditor what your plans are. **This will not help your cause.**

SETTLING YOUR FIRST CARD

When is the right time to settle my first account and how do I go about doing that?

The right time to start working on settlement is once you have become at least 6 months delinquent on your accounts, and you have saved at least 30% of your smallest card. You want to work off of the balance that your card was when you chose to go delinquent. I understand that you have accrued interest and late fees, but when you are talking to the creditor you are going to want to offer 18-20% of the balance that your card was before you went delinquent.

For Example:	Your initial balance before going delinquent	$10,000
	You are going to offer	$1,800

****Always Start Out Lower Than You Want To Settle The Account For****

Now there is typically going to be some negotiations to come to an agreement that both you and the creditor are comfortable with. What you must remember is that it is important for you to get the best deal you can, so that you can spend the least amount of money possible to settle all of your debts. The lower the percentage (%) you agree to the least amount of money it will cost you to become debt free.

****Sometimes you need to stand strong****

It will be very rare that you call the creditor and they accept your initial offer. It doesn't mean that they can't do what you are asking them to do. It simply means they think they can get more out of you and are going to tell you that they can't do it. Sometimes it is best to let them know that this is all the money you have and that is all you can do. You may also let them know that you are getting ready to call another one of your creditors and that you are going to settle the account with the creditor that gives you the best settlement offer. Also let them know that once you spend this money on your first settlement that it is going to take quite a while for you to have any more funds available for settlement and maybe they should go ahead and take what you have to offer. If they still refuse and you have offered them all the way up to what you are comfortable with then you can politely tell them that if they change their mind to give you a call. You will be surprised how **standing strong,** can get you a great settlement!

So Let's Review

1. Tell them this is all the money you have

2. You are prepared to call another creditor

3. Your money will go to creditor that offers the smallest amount

4. You are not happy with offer tell them you will call them another time

5. Stand Strong!

What to do once they agree to a settlement.

Once you have come to terms on a settlement with a particular creditor you want to **get that agreement in writing.** You do not want to give them your bank account information to draft the agreed upon settlement until they have provided you with a **Settlement Letter**. This settlement letter should read that you have agreed upon a certain dollar amount and that this account will be considered paid in full, or paid as agreed on your credit report once they receive the money. This settlement letter should also give the date on which they plan to withdraw any funds from your account.

So Let's Review

1. Come to terms

2. Get agreement in writing this is Settlement Letter

3. Don't give them your bank draft information until you get a Settlement Letter

4. Review Settlement Letter

5. Settlement Letter shows Paid in Full or Paid as Agreed!

SETTLING CARD #2 – LAST

****Always Start Out Lower Than You Want To Settle the Account For****

Now there is typically going to be some negotiations to come to an agreement that both you and the creditor are comfortable with. What you must remember is that it is important for you to get the best deal you can, so that you can spend the least amount of money possible to settle all of your debts. The lower the percentage (%) you agree to the least amount of money it will cost you to become debt free.

****Sometimes you need to stand strong****

It will be very rare that you call the creditor and they accept your initial offer. It doesn't mean that they can't do what you are asking them to do. It simply means they think they can get more out of you and are going to tell you that they can't do it. Sometimes it is best to let them know that this is all the money you have and that is all you can do. You may also let them know that you are getting ready to call another one of your creditors and that you are going to settle the account with the creditor that gives you the best settlement offer. Also let them know that once you spend this money on your first settlement that it is going to take quite a while for you to have any more funds available for settlement and maybe they should go ahead and take what you have to offer. If they still refuse and you have offered them all the way up to what you are comfortable with then you can politely tell them that if they change their mind to give you a call. You will be surprised how **standing strong,** can get you a great settlement!

So Let's Review

1. Tell them this is all the money you have

2. You are prepared to call another creditor

3. Your money will go to creditor that offers the smallest amount

4. You are not happy with offer tell them you will call them another time

5. Stand Strong!

What to do once they agree to a settlement.

Once you have come to terms on a settlement with a particular creditor you want to **get that agreement in writing.** You do not want to give them your bank account information to draft the agreed upon settlement until they have provided you with a **Settlement Letter**. This settlement letter should read that you have agreed upon a certain dollar amount and that this account will be considered paid in full, or paid as agreed on your credit report once they receive the money. This settlement letter should also give the date on which they plan to withdraw any funds from your account.

So Let's Review

1. Come to terms

2. Get agreement in writing this is Settlement Letter

3. Don't give them your bank draft information until you get a Settlement Letter

4. Review Settlement Letter

5. Settlement Letter shows Paid in Full or Paid as Agreed!

HANDELING DIFFICULT CREDITORS

Be prepared. Have a calculator, Pen and Paper and the most recent Statement for each card.

One of the first things that you need to remember when speaking with your creditors is they will know everything about your situation (your payment history on anything that you have on your credit report, mortgage information, medical information, car payments, student loans etc.). They have access to get your employment information past and present. You don't want to engage in any conversation in regards to those things. You never have to tell them where you work and how long you have been there at all. They will try and trick you into filling out information to pin you against a wall.

When calling to settle an account, do not talk to them about anything other than that one card. There are a few key things that you want to ask up front so that you can have the best tool in negotiating.

- **What is my current balance?**

Always remember you do not owe the person you are talking to on the other line anything! You owe the bank that issued the credit card. Do not let the collector on the other end of the phone scare you into something just because he is feeding you the "truth" about your financial situation. Sure you may have lost your job but you are still paying mortgage payments, day-care and car payments.

When the conversation starts getting off track (which would be anything other than discussing a settlement) quickly remind them that you are calling to **SETTLE** this card. They might say a few of the following:

- **Well your account is not eligible for a settlement at this time.**

Ask when your account will be eligible? If the answer is I don't know but we can set you up on an interest free program with a payment that you can afford whatever that may be. Kindly say **No Thank You!** I will call back later. **Hang the Phone Up!** They will keep calling and you must be persistent in stating that you are only willing to settle.

- **You are not delinquent enough**

If a creditor tells you that you are not delinquent enough simply say "okay when was the last date that you received a payment from me"? They will respond and then you can ask them how many days that is. I usually respond back with "hmm I haven't paid you in 90 days I guess I will wait another 90 days. Thank you and then **Hang Up!** They will keep calling.

If you can maintain your "other" payments (mortgage, car payments and so on) why can't you pay this debt

If the person on the other line is talking about how you appear to be able to maintain multiple car payments, mortgage payments, money to put food on the table for your family. Simply say "Sir with all due respect don't you have to put food on your table for you and your children and have a place to sleep at night" let's get back to the point of this call. Can we please discuss a settlement on my account, what did you say the current balance was? If that still doesn't work I would ask them if there is a supervisor a can speak with.

Never let them bully you out of what you are offering, start out really low and if they laugh at you or say well you charged more than that on the card respond with this. "Okay what is it that you are wanting for a settlement"?

<u>Remember you do not want to take anything over 50% of the current balance?</u>

Be careful they will use phrases such as this well I can waive 30% off your debt for you that's a great deal.

NO it's not a great deal you are still paying back 70% of what you owe.

Also remember that the letters that are sent to you in the mail 95% of the time you can get them to come down much lower than the offer they sent to you.

Also keep in my mind that the letters will have an expiration date on them usually 30 days from the date it was sent. If you call them and they say well I sent that to you last month or it expired yesterday the offer is higher now. <u>Don't believe that.</u> Be persistent and just say "oh well okay I will call another one of my creditors and put you guys to the back of the list".

If they are giving you a hard time even if it's the only card that you have tell them that you have 10 more cards and they can quickly be the last card you choose to settle.

Another thing to remember is your hardship; even if you are just tired of paying all this debt, talk up your hardship stress the fact that you have a hard time paying all of the things to keep your family going.

LEGAL ISSUES

There is a chance that during this process you will receive legal action against you. This will be served to you by a process server in the form of a legal document titled a Summons or Citation. If this does happen just sign for the document and take a deep breath. You can get through this.

You cannot go to jail for a credit card debt nor can they take your home away. These are all real emotions that you will be feeling.

There are a few things that I would like you to do. Grab a pen, paper, your card statement for this account and a calculator.

You need to read through this document thoroughly.

The standard flow of a summons is this:

1. You receive a summons

2. You send your written response

3. Judgment

4. Stipulated Agreement for Settlement/ Stipulated Agreement for Payment Arrangement.

I like to explain a judgment as this; it's like an insurance policy between you and the creditor it will be filed with the county court house and stay there until you settle this account. If you default in a payment to the law firm or creditor it will allow them to take further legal action. It's standard to receive a judgment in this process.

To keep it from becoming a default judgment you will need to send out your response to the court so that you are complying with the laws of your state.

The following list will tell you step by step what to do to comply with this action.

- You have 30 days to respond (some citations will have only 20 days)

    - A response to the court does not mean that you have to appear in court; you can respond and should respond to this document immediately in the form of a written answer.

- o This can be typed or handwritten with the following information. You must include in this letter the following

    - The name of the court division that is on the top of your summons, your case number which is typically on the upper right hand side of the document, your full name, address and the creditor of whom you were served by.

    - A brief hardship of how and why you are in this situation and a short response letting them know that you are saving towards taking care of this debt. I also include that any further action against me would be detrimental to my family.

    - You must send this response to the county courthouse and the law firm that is representing the creditor. All of this information will be on your summons.

There is always something that can be done on a legal account. You can settle or you can set it on a Payment Arrangement.

- Locate the name of the attorney firm that is handling this summons. This is typically found in two places. Either the first page in the upper left hand corner or the very last page of the summons where the signature line is. Write down this phone number. You will now be calling them to discuss your account. Just like in the previous section on handling difficult creditors they will bombard you with numerous questions on why you have not paid the debt owed. It is very important that when speaking with the law office in regards to a summons you are polite but to the point.

- Ask them what the current balance on the account is. Write this down on your paper. Begin to ask them what we can do to settle this card. The first response they give you is typically not the lowest offer they can give. You can negotiate a summons without giving them your financials (pay check stubs, bank information). If they start out around 80% of your balance write that down. Take your time don't let them rush you into making any kind of decision. I would evaluate your balance and your savings that you have

- accumulated and figure out what 30% of the balance is. You always want to offer them low low low. You never want to offer the max of what you want to pay.

- Never give them a set amount that you can pay monthly they will hold you to this. Always speak as if you don't have the funds and that you are really going to have to try and save or borrower. This leaves you with the upper hand in negotiating.

If you see that the balance on this account is larger than what your accumulated savings can handle at this point you can talk about the other option like a payment arrangement on the balance in full with the option to settle the account at a later date?

What is a payment arrangement? A payment arrangement is monthly payment plan set up through the law firm and typically filed with the court system on the entire balance. This can consist of a down payment of some kind and the lowest monthly payment you can get. Other times a down payment is not required. I would suggest that you start negotiating without a down payment and try to get the monthly payment to something you feel comfortable with. The point of a down payment is to lower your monthly payment.

Example. If they suggest paying $200.00 a month and you feel this needs to be lower ask them if giving a down payment would get this to $150.00. they will respond with sure you can put 1000.00 down however your monthly payment will only be $185.00 this would not be worth giving them all that cash up front to only save $15.00 a month. (You can use that $1000.00 on a different card)

- When coming up with a payment arrangement you may have to give them a little more information. This is normal. You have to show the law firm and the creditor that you are experiencing financial troubles and cannot come up with the funds to settle. I would strongly suggest that you stay away from sending them or verbally giving them the name of your bank or your employer.

- When you agree on a payment plan ask them to fax, email or mail the agreement to your home. You will need to sign this and send it back to the law firm. Please remember to keep a copy of any and all documents you receive.

- When agreeing to a payment arrangement you need to ask them if I can come back at any time and settle this account. The answer is YES!

If you cannot come up with an agreement for settlement or arrangement with the law firm you can request a court date to go before the judge and explain your situation. This should be worst case scenario. Almost 100% of the time you will be able to come up with an agreement with the law firm without having to do this.

If you do have to go to court be prepared. Bring all the documentation that you have discussed with the firm what they offer, what you offered and your hardship letter and list of expenses.

Part 1

BUDGET WORKSHEET

CATEGORY	MONTHLY BUDGET AMOUNT	MONTHLY ACTUAL AMOUNT	DIFFERENCE
INCOME:			
Wages and Bonuses			
Interest Income			
Investment Income			
Miscellaneous Income			
Income Subtotal			
INCOME TAXES WITHHELD:			
Federal Income Tax			
State and Local Income Tax			
Social Security/Medicare Tax			
Income Taxes Subtotal			
Spendable Income			
EXPENSES:			
HOME:			
Mortgage or Rent			
Homeowners/Renters Insurance			
Property Taxes			
Home Repairs/Maintenance/HOA Dues			
Home Improvements			
UTILITIES:			
Electricity			
Water and Sewer			
Natural Gas or Oil			
Telephone (Land Line, Cell)			
FOOD:			
Groceries			
Eating Out, Lunches, Snacks			
FAMILY OBLIGATIONS:			
Child Support			
Alimony			
Day Care, Babysitting			

Part 2

BUDGET WORKSHEET	MONTHLY BUDGET AMOUNT	MONTHLY ACTUAL AMOUNT	
CATEGORY			DIFFERENCE
HEALTH AND MEDICAL:			
Insurance (Medical, Dental, Vision)			
Fitness (Yoga, Massage, Gym)			
TRANSPORTATION:			
Car Payments			
Gasoline/Oil			
Auto Repairs/Maintenance/Fees			
Auto Insurance			
Other Transportation (tolls,bus,subway,taxis)			
DEBT PAYMENTS:			
Credit Cards			
Student Loans			
Other Loans			
ENTERTAINMENT/RECREATION:			
Cable TV/Videos/Movies			
Computer Expenses			
Hobbies			
PETS:			
Food, Grooming, Boarding, Vet			
CLOTHING:			
INVESTMENTS AND SAVINGS:			
401 (k) or IRA			
Stocks/Bonds/Mutual Funds			
College Fund			
MISCELLANEOUS:			
Toiletries, Household Products			
Gifts/Donations			
Grooming (Hair, Make-up, Other)			
Miscellaneous Expenses			
Total Investments and Expenses			
Surplus or Shortage (Spendable income minus total expenses and investments)			

www.ingramcontent.com/pod-product-compliance
Lightning Source LLC
Chambersburg PA
CBHW071603170526
45166CB00004B/1777